First published by Parragon in 2013
Parragon
Chartist House
15–17 Trim Street
Bath BA1 1HA, UK
www.parragon.com

Copyright © 2013 Disney Enterprises, Inc.

All rights reserved. No part of this publication may be reproduced, stored in a retrieval system or transmitted, in any form or by any means, electronic, mechanical, photocopying, recording or otherwise, without the prior permission of the copyright holder.

ISBN 978-1-4723-1932-6

Printed in China

Contents

Character Profiles	8
The Story of the Movie	20
Your Movie Star Profile	42
Quiz – Surf vs. Turf	44
Learn the Lingo!	46
Party Time!	48
Fab Friends	64
Totally Secret	72
Quiz – Get into the Groove	88
Make a Memory Box	90
That was Awesome!	92

MACK

"Girls can do anything boys can do ... and we look better doing it!"

Mack is one awesome *wahine* (that's Hawaiian for 'girl')! She can rip on the biggest waves, she's super-smart in school and she's a fantastic friend. Mack has big dreams and great friends to help her find her destiny.

NAME: McKenzie

ALSO KNOWN AS: Mack

LIKES: Surfing

LOVES: The beach, especially Grandpa's beach surf shop

DISLIKES: Being trapped in an old movie

DREAM: To ride a huge wave

Brady is Mack's best friend and boyfriend. He knows what he wants and isn't afraid of what anyone else thinks. Brady never gives up on his dreams or his friends.

NAME: Brady

ALSO KNOWN AS: "Knight in shining board shorts"

LIKES: *Wet Side Story,* an old surfing movie, and cheesy lines from movies

LOVES: Surfing with Mack and hanging out at the beach

DISLIKES: When Mack keeps secrets from him

DREAM: To be in a movie like *Wet Side Story*

LELA

"I know bikers aren't supposed to like surfing, but I don't care."

Lela is one seriously cool biker living in the movie, *Wet Side Story*. Her brother, Butchy, is the leader of the biker gang, but Lela has secretly always wanted to try surfing. She is fabulous, feisty and knows how to be a friend forever.

NAME: Lela

LIKES: Hanging out at Big Momma's with her friends

LOVES: Slumber parties

DISLIKES: Having to keep her dream a secret from her brother

DREAM: To learn how to surf

TANNER

"If I was going to think something right now, I think I'd think that maybe people aren't always what I think."

Tanner can carry a tune and a surfboard! He can rhyme, rip a wave and riff on the guitar, and he's a great friend. This super-cute surfin' dude from *Wet Side Story* doesn't always say things just right, but he's pretty smart (sometimes more pretty than smart).

NAME: Tanner

LIKES: Playing the guitar

LOVES: Surfing

DISLIKES: The biker gang

DREAM: To find the right girl – someone really special

The surf-and-turf war is hotting up between the Rodents (the bikers) and the surfers. When Mack and Brady find themselves at Big Momma's, it's easy to see that the groups do not get along.

LEADER: Butchy

HANG OUT: Big Momma's Bungalow

SIDE OF THE RESTAURANT: Left

Struts

CheeChee

THE SURFERS

"Why don't you (Rodents) make like the ocean and wave goodbye?"

The surfer gang don't think the bikers could ever stand up on a surfboard. And this wave-loving bunch definitely do not find bikes cool at all!

LEADER:
Tanner

HANG OUT:
Big Momma's Bungalow

SIDE OF THE RESTAURANT:
Right

Rascal

The Story of the Movie

The sun shone brightly on a California beach on a perfect surfing day. The conditions were just right for catching waves. McKenzie – Mack to her friends – loved surfing. She had spent the whole summer at the beach, living at her grandfather's surf shop and hanging out with her boyfriend, Brady.

After a few hours of surfing, a stunning sunset spread out across the sky. Brady looked over at Mack and grinned. "Best day ever!" he exclaimed.

Mack smiled, but she had a secret. Tomorrow her Aunt Antoinette was coming to take her away to attend a private school. Mack just couldn't find the words to tell Brady that she was leaving.

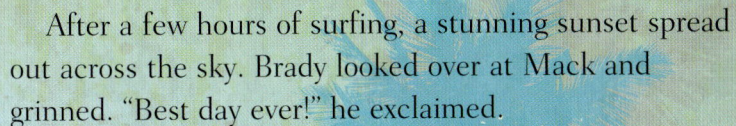

Before Mack had the chance to break the bad news, Aunt Antoinette arrived – a day early! She had booked them onto a flight the next morning.

Brady was upset. "How can you leave?" he asked Mack.

Mack tried to explain. "After we lost my mum, the deal was I would stay here with my grandfather through the first part of high school. Then, when it was time to get more serious, I'd go to this school, like my aunt did."

The next morning, Mack headed out for a last-minute surf. She couldn't leave without one more ride. Her grandfather and Brady watched from the beach.

It was aggressive surf, but Mack expertly ripped across each wave. And when she saw a huge wave building, she headed straight for it. Brady was worried. He jumped on a Jet Ski and raced out to stop her.

As the wave broke, Mack and Brady both disappeared under the water....

Mack and Brady both came up, gasping for air. They made their way to the shore and staggered onto the beach.

Everything looked ... different. Who were those boys singing? And why was everyone wearing 1960s beachwear?

"Okay," Mack said slowly, feeling very confused. "I must have hit my head. Is this what a concussion looks like?"

"Did we both hit our heads?" Brady asked, as a chorus of dancers headed their way.

Brady soon realized what was going on. As strange as it was, the action happening around them was from his favourite movie, a musical called *Wet Side Story*!

Brady pulled Mack towards a beach-hut restaurant called Big Momma's. Inside there were two groups – the surfers and the Rodents, who were bikers. Recalling the plot of the movie, Brady leaned in to Mack. "Each gang wants the other gone so they can have this place for themselves."

"So," said Mack. "We landed in the middle of a surf-and-turf war?"

Later, one of the biker girls, Lela, sang onstage. Mack sighed and turned to leave, and bumped right into a surfer guy, Tanner. They locked gazes.

At the same time, across the room, Lela suddenly stumbled and fell off the stage. Brady rushed over and caught her. Lela flashed him a smile. "I guess I literally fell for you, huh?" she cooed.

Lela and Tanner were the two main characters in *Wet Side Story*, and they were meant to fall for each other. Now they'd fallen for Mack and Brady instead!

"We changed the movie," Brady told Mack.

Mack was worried. There was meant to be a storm at the end of the movie, which she had hoped would help them get home. Now the storm might not happen!

Brady told Mack about the bad guy from *Wet Side Story*, Les Camembert. In the movie, he built a machine to change the weather and make the surfers and bikers leave the beach so that he could build a resort there. The storm only happened when Lela and Tanner got together, united the rival gangs and destroyed that machine!

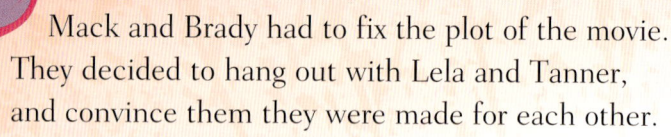

Mack and Brady had to fix the plot of the movie. They decided to hang out with Lela and Tanner, and convince them they were made for each other.

Mack went to the biker girls' pyjama party in Lela's bedroom. The girls styled each other's hair and talked about boys. It was a very girly evening!

Meanwhile, Brady hung out with Tanner and the surfer guys. He dropped Lela into the conversation.

"The Rodent?" a surfer called Seacat said. "We don't date no rats."

"You wouldn't take out a girl just because she's a biker?" Brady asked.

"Don't listen to those guys," Tanner said, leaning close to him. "It don't matter if a girl's a surfer, a biker or a bookworm." Brady smiled. There was still hope!

The next day, Mack chatted to Tanner. She asked him why there was such a conflict between the surfers and bikers. Shrugging, Tanner said, "It's how it's supposed to be, I guess. Like, it's sort of what everyone expects."

Tanner's reply made Mack think. "It's like your heart tells you one thing, but you feel like you have to do something else," she said.

"That's why people who don't follow their hearts, leave their hearts behind," Tanner said.

Later on, Mack was back in Lela's bedroom. The two were becoming good friends. Suddenly, Lela scurried over to Mack. "I have a secret I've never told anyone!" She closed her eyes tightly. "I want to surf."

"Surf? Really!" Mack exclaimed.

Lela knew it sounded crazy. Her brother was the leader of the biker gang and would blow a gasket if he found out!

"Lela," said Mack. "Never let anyone tell you that you can't do what you want in life."

Then Mack had a great idea – Brady could teach Lela to surf. This could get Tanner to notice Lela!

But things got a lot worse the next day. Mack and Brady were starting to morph into the movie! They couldn't stop themselves singing their feelings. When Mack emerged from the ocean with her hair still dry, she knew they had to do something – fast!

"Let's go find Lela and Tanner," Brady suggested. "We have to get them together so they can find out about Les's weather machine and then unify everyone to destroy it before it destroys them!"

"Oh no! We're talking in plot points," Mack cried.

They began to run but stopped short when Les and Dr Fusion appeared in front of them, blocking their way.

Les marched Mack and Brady to his secret laboratory in a nearby lighthouse, and tied them up. He didn't want them trying to ruin his plan.

They were left alone, and Mack began talking. She admitted she didn't really want to go to private school. She tilted her head towards Brady. "You were right. What's my hurry to grow up when I could be stuck in 1962 with you?"

Brady slipped his hand into Mack's. They didn't know what would happen next, but they were happy to be together.

Back on the beach, Lela was looking for Brady – they had arranged a surfing lesson. Tanner was there too, searching for Mack.

"You waiting for Brady?" Tanner asked Lela.

"Yeah," Lela said. "We're going to surf."

"What? You like to surf?" Tanner asked, surprised.

"I know bikers aren't supposed to like surfing, but I don't care," Lela cried.

"You don't?" Tanner asked. He moved closer to her. The biker chick he had seen hanging around Big Momma's suddenly looked different to him. "Hey. You know what? I've always wanted to ride a motorcycle," he confessed.

Suddenly, they started to sing about destiny and belonging together. They looked into each other's eyes ... and kissed.

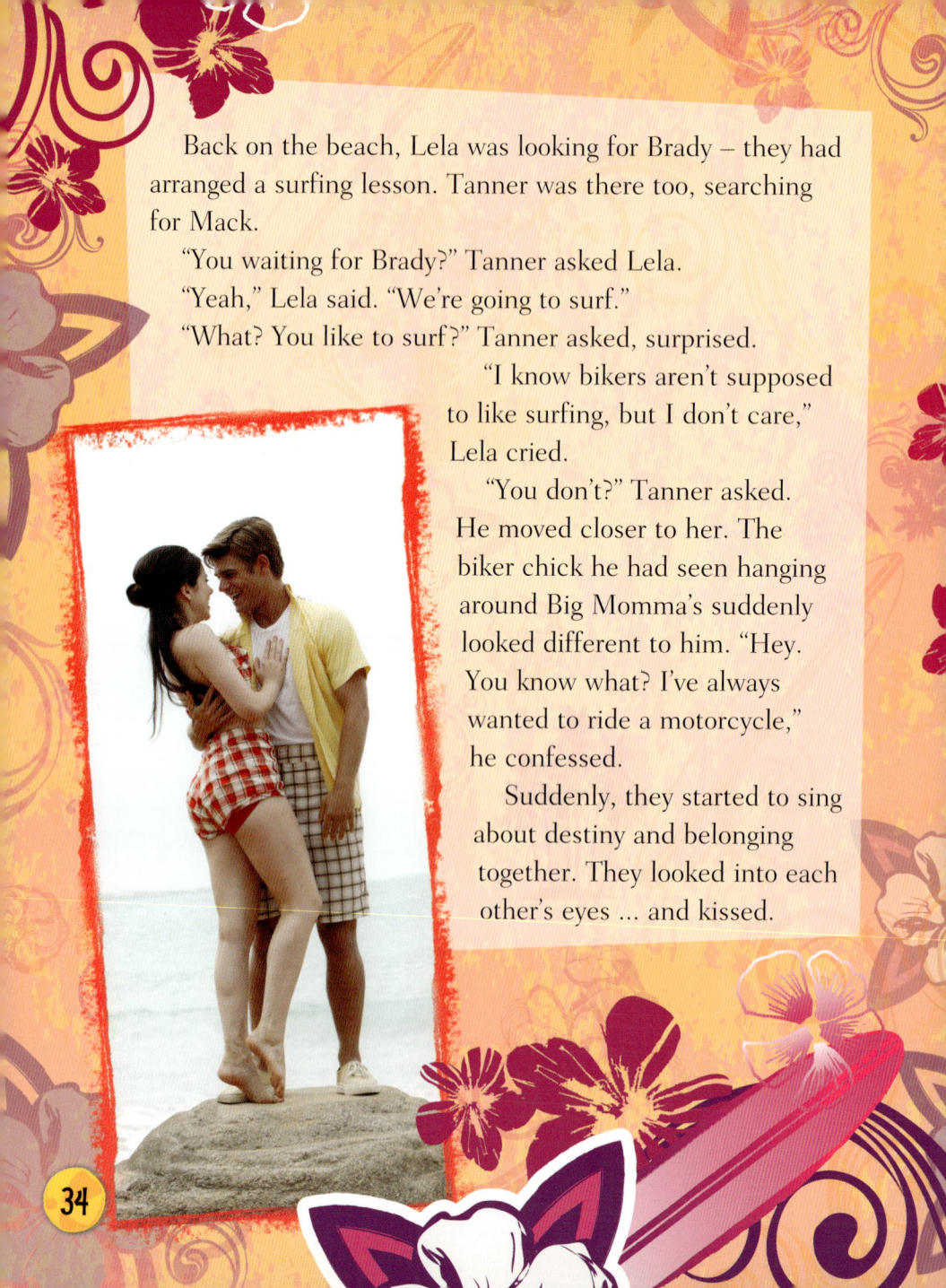

"What are we going to tell Mack and Brady?" Lela asked.

"Yeah, where are they anyway?" Tanner said. Looking around, he spotted a flower garland on the sand. Mack had been wearing it. "Something's not right!" he cried.

They looked at each other and then towards the lighthouse in the distance. Suddenly, everything clicked into place. They remembered the crazy property developer who had once tried to bribe them to leave Big Momma's. The new couple raced up the beach to find help. They needed to figure out how to save Mack and Brady!

Tanner and Lela burst into Big Momma's and leaped onto the stage. There was complete silence as everyone watched the mismatched pair – a surfer boy and a biker chick. The couple told everyone about needing to rescue Mack and Brady and save the beach.

"The only hope is to work together," Tanner urged.

After a long moment of silence, Butchy – the leader of the Rodents – approached Tanner and shook his hand.

"Let's go!" Butchy and Tanner shouted in unison. They led the crowd out of the restaurant, down the beach towards the lighthouse. They were on a mission. And now they were all united!

When the gang arrived at the lighthouse, they took Les and Dr Fusion by surprise. Mack and Brady noticed that Lela and Tanner were holding hands.

"Look at that, Brady," Mack said. "They got together all by themselves."

Brady grinned. "I guess they had to. It was written that way."

The surfers and bikers quickly turned the tables on Les and Dr Fusion. Lela found a way to short-circuit the weather machine. But suddenly, there was a low rumble.

"Let's get out of here!" Butchy yelled.

Everyone escaped the laboratory just before the weather machine exploded. The two bad guys went flying and landed out in the ocean, bobbing in the water.

Mack and Brady suddenly found themselves back outside Big Momma's.

"How did we get back here?" Mack asked.

"Because it's exactly where we're supposed to be," Brady replied. "We can leave exactly as we came."

Lela, Tanner and the others arrived and everyone sadly said their goodbyes.

Tanner ran and fetched Mack's surfboard. He tried to convince them to stay, telling them it was always perfect there. Mack nodded her head. "Where I'm going back to is perfect also," she said. She took Brady's hand and gave it a tight squeeze. "I'm going to make sure of it."

"You sure you're ready?" Brady whispered.

"Yeah," she said, "now that I know what I'm going home to do."

She was going to miss everyone, but she had never been more ready to go home.

Everyone on the beach waved as Mack and Brady paddled out towards the incoming waves. The ocean was rumbling with the sound of crashing water. There was a storm coming.

A huge wave rose up and the two were there to meet it just in time. As they surfed through the barrel, the wave crashed down on them, pulling the pair deep beneath the swirling water.

When they resurfaced, Mack realized her hair was wet. That meant they were home!

"Hey," Brady said to Mack. "No time has passed. This is exactly when we left!"

"We did it!" Mack cheered.

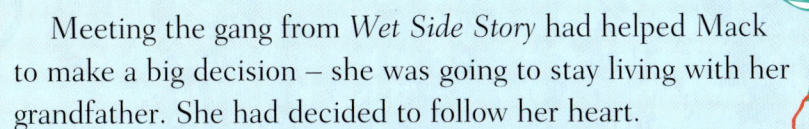

Meeting the gang from *Wet Side Story* had helped Mack to make a big decision – she was going to stay living with her grandfather. She had decided to follow her heart.

"I want to finish high school here," Mack told her aunt. "I want to be with Brady, surf more and enjoy myself. Then, well, I don't know what then," she said, laughing. "The thing is, I don't have to know. Not just yet. But whatever it is, it'll be my choice."

Aunt Antoinette understood. She hugged her niece.

"See!" Mack cried. "Who doesn't love a movie with a happy ending?" She turned to look at her grandfather, Aunt Antoinette and Brady. There was no other place in the world she'd rather be!

The End

Fill in your own MOVIE STAR PROFILE!

Write your own movie-star bio:
_____
_____
_____
_____
_____
_____
_____
_____
_____
_____
_____
_____

Star facts about you:

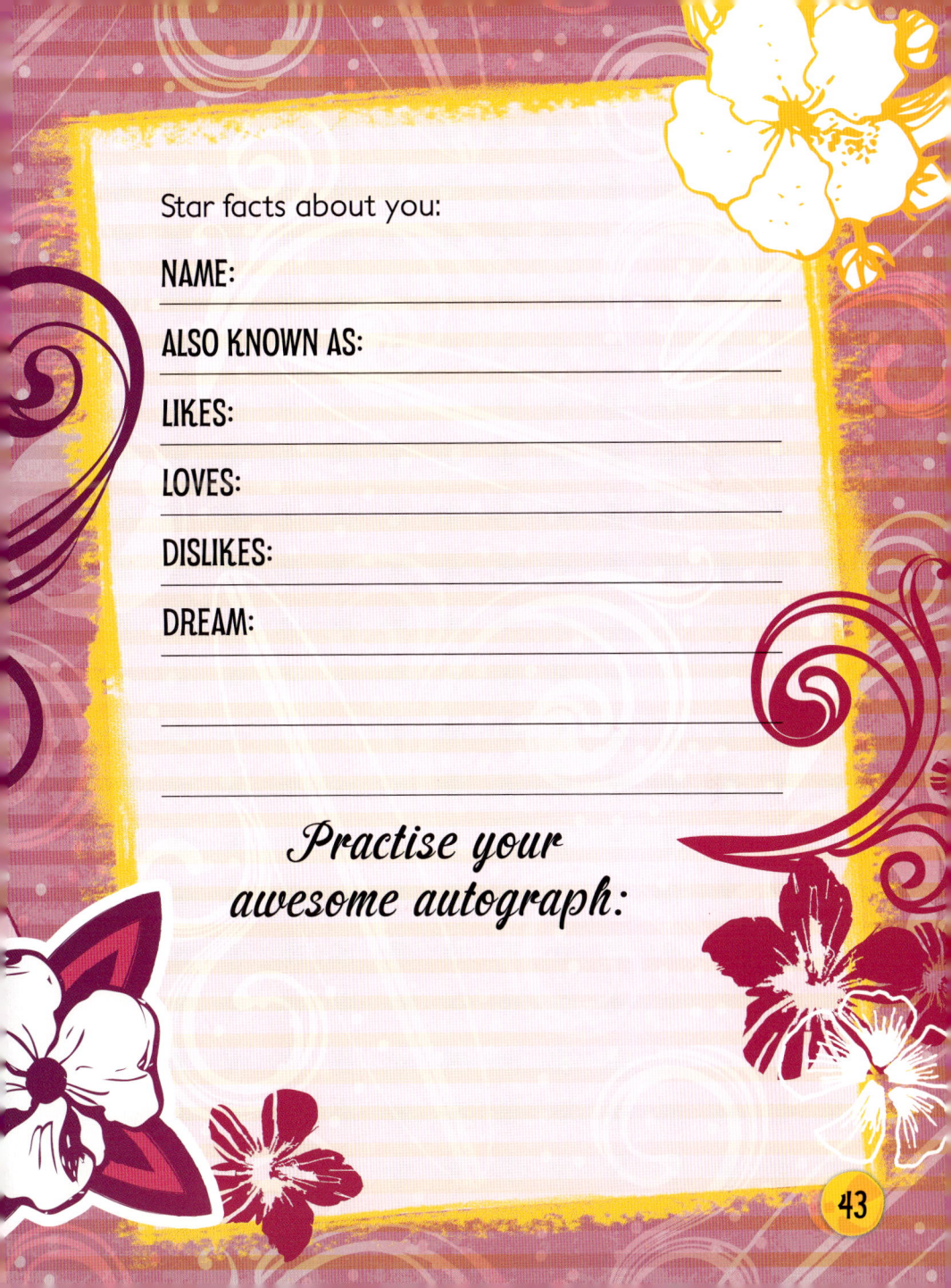

NAME:

ALSO KNOWN AS:

LIKES:

LOVES:

DISLIKES:

DREAM:

Practise your awesome autograph:

SURF vs. TURF

When Mack and Brady land in *Wet Side Story*, it's bikers versus surfers. Which team would you be on? Take the quiz to find out. Then, check out your result.

1. IF I COULD HANG OUT ANYWHERE IT WOULD BE ...
   A. the beach
   B. the park
   C. I like both

2. LEATHER JACKETS ARE ...
   A. not for me
   B. so totally cool
   C. okay — I could wear one

3. THE SPORT I'M BETTER AT IS ...
   A. swimming
   B. cycling
   C. any sport

4. MY BIKE IS ...
   A. still in the garage (I've never used it!)
   B. my favourite way to get around
   C. used, but not every day

5. IF I COULD DECORATE A SURFBOARD, I WOULD ...
   A. design the coolest pattern ever
   B. surfboard? I don't want one
   C. doesn't really matter as long as it works

IF YOU ANSWERED ...

MOSTLY As: Surf's up! Wild waves are like your best friends. You'd rather be on a sandy beach than on a bike any day. Kowabunga!

MOSTLY Bs: Super biker! Zooming around on your bike is totally groovy to you. You might think surfing is all washed up.

MOSTLY Cs: All-rounder! An amazing athlete and all-round person. Like Mack and Brady, you know you can be anything you want to be.

LEARN THE LINGO!

Talk like the gang from *Wet Side Story*! Here are some quality quotes....

Kibosh

Shreddin' the Wave

Carvin' the Barrel

Far Out!

Ho-dads

Awesome!

Sounds blastin'

Pretty groovy

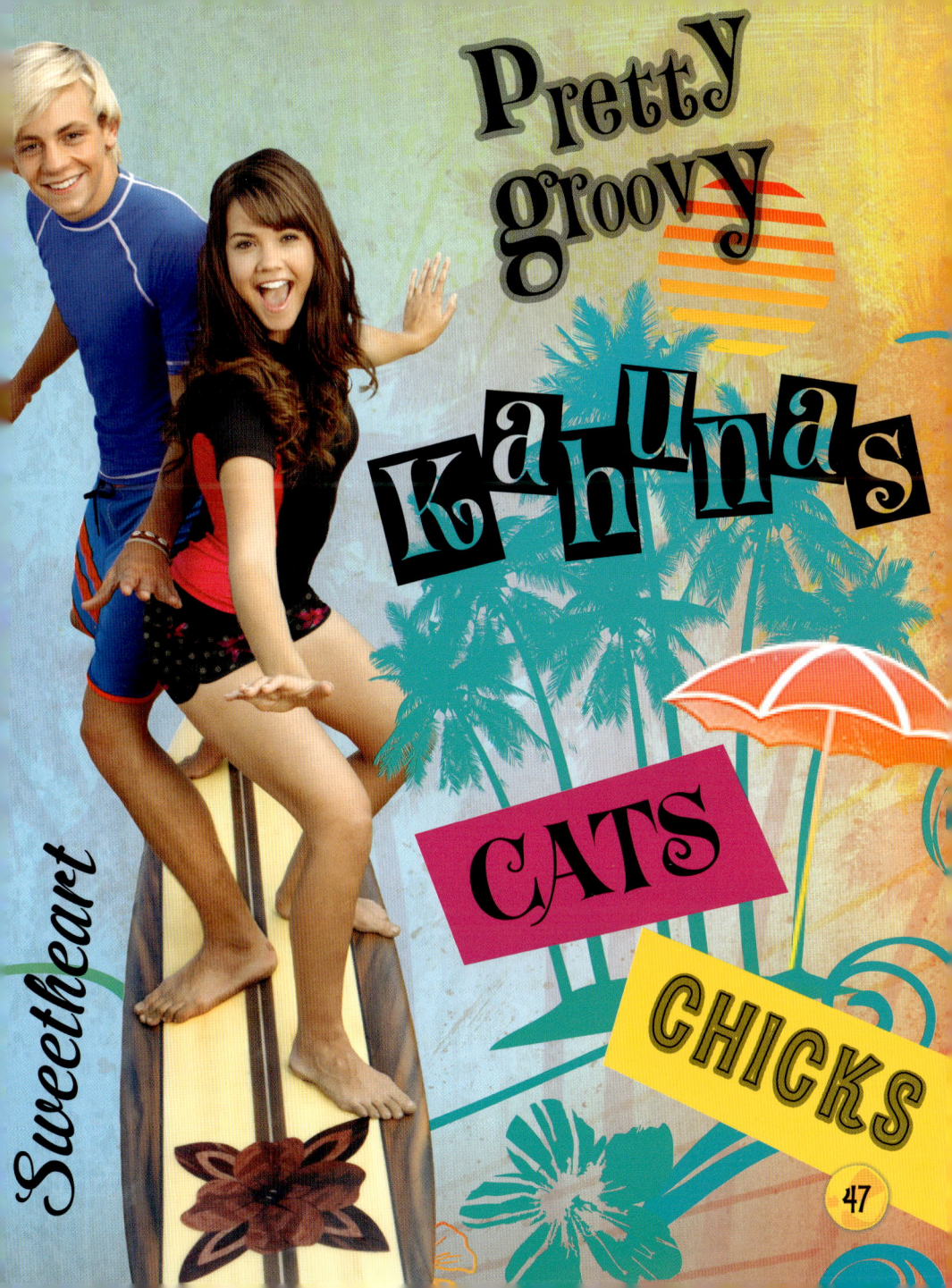

Kahunas

Cats

Chicks

Sweetheart

47

PARTY TIME!

Lela invites Mack to a slumber party. She has never been to one before. Have you?

"I've never had a pyjama party!"

Mack, Lela and the girls spend the night chatting and playing vintage records.

LIST 10 TOTALLY TERRIFIC THINGS YOU'D DO AT A SLUMBER PARTY:

1. _____
2. _____
3. _____
4. _____
5. _____
6. _____
7. _____
8. _____
9. _____
10. _____

PARTY PLANNER

Lela has slumber parties all the time – she's a pro! Prep for your own party on these pages.

Guest list

_____

_____

_____

_____

_____

_____

_____

_____

_____

_____

VENUE:

MOVIES TO WATCH:

1.

2.

3.

SNACKS:

GAMES TO PLAY:

INSANELY COOL INVITATIONS

You'll need a super special invitation for your slumber party! Fill in all the details below.

YOU'RE INVITED TO _____'S
(YOUR NAME)

Super Secret Slumber Party

WHERE: _____

WHEN: _____

PLEASE RESPOND TO _____

BY _____

Now create a cool design for the reverse side of your invitation. Let your imagination go wild! Then photocopy these pages to create as many invitations as you need.

AWESOME ADDRESSES

Before you can send your invitations, you'll need to have your BFFs' addresses. Hopefully none of them have been transported back in time by a super storm!

NAME:
ADDRESS:
PHONE:
E-MAIL:

NAME:
ADDRESS:
PHONE:
E-MAIL:

NAME:
ADDRESS:
PHONE:
E-MAIL:

NAME:
ADDRESS:
PHONE:
E-MAIL:

NAME:
ADDRESS:
PHONE:
E-MAIL:

NAME:
ADDRESS:
PHONE:
E-MAIL:

SO THIS IS A *Shindig?*

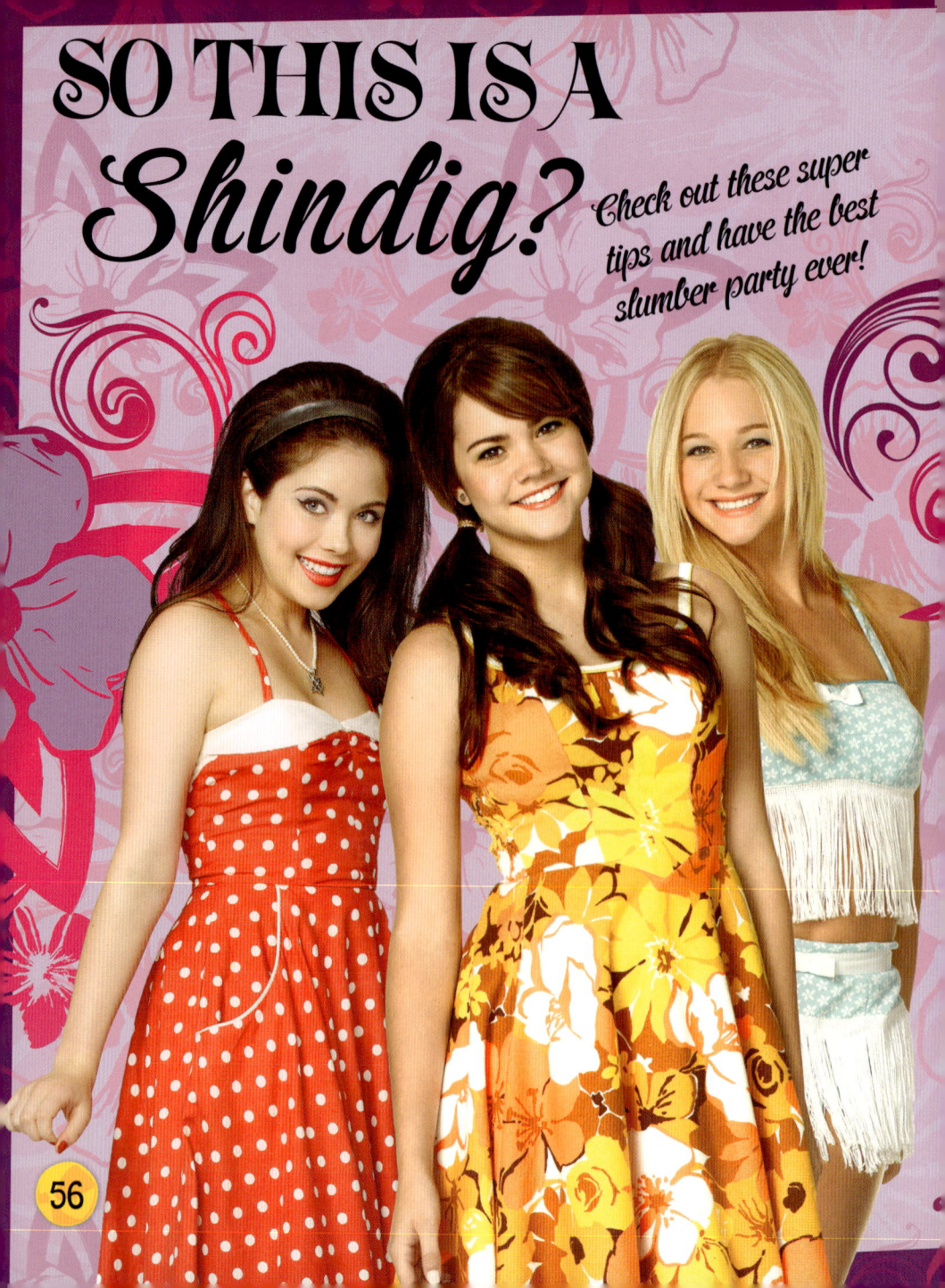

Check out these super tips and have the best slumber party ever!

RIDIN' ON THE WILD SIDE:
Stock up on sweets and snacks! Find out what your friends' favourite treats are and head to the shops. It's a party – live on the wild side!

TIME TO PLAY:
Whether you love board games, video games or even want to invent your own games, it's time to play. If you're stuck for ideas, charades and Truth or Dare are slumber party classics.

EVERY MINUTE WE'RE HERE, WE'RE TOGETHER:
Slumber parties are perfect for sharing secrets and chatting with your BFFs!

WE'RE IN A MOVIE:
Okay, so you might not be in a movie, but you can definitely watch some. Show your fave movie to your friends and find out what they think!

TOO CUTE TO BE DANGEROUS:
Slumber parties are for pampering. Grab some outfits for fancy dress, create some crazy cool hair-dos and even paint your nails.

SPEED AND WHEELS AND ROCK 'N' ROLL:
Rock out to your favourite beats – sing, dance and laugh with your best friends.

SLEEPOVER SING-OFF

Sleepovers are great for singing!
Have a sing-off with your friends. Here's how:

List your five fave songs below. Each person sings one song, or you can sing together! Rate each performance using the scale below and fill in the table on the opposite page. The winner is the singer with the most points.

PRETTY AWESOME – 1 POINT
TOTALLY FAR OUT – 2 POINTS
SERIOUSLY GROOVY! – 3 POINTS

Your fave songs:

1. _____
2. _____
3. _____
4. _____
5. _____

Star Scores!

NAME:	SCORE:
1.	
2.	
3.	
4.	
5.	

COOL Seaside BASH

Turn your room into a beach-inspired paradise for your next slumber party. Here's how:

PLAY SOME BEACH TUNES – TROPICAL MUSIC OR EVEN THE SOUND OF WAVES CRASHING ON THE SHORE WILL DO.

LAY TOWELS OVER EACH GIRL'S BED OR SLEEPING BAG. IT'S BEACH LIFE!

GIVE EVERYONE A PAIR OF SUNGLASSES FOR THE NIGHT AND PRETEND YOU'RE ON THE BEACH!

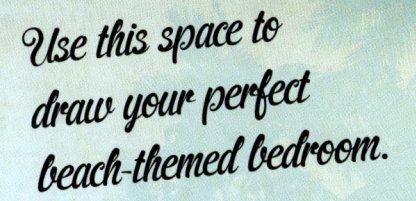

Use this space to draw your perfect beach-themed bedroom.

RELAX, DANCE AND HAVE FUN – JUST LIKE THE SURFERS AND THE BIKERS!

Fab Fashion Show

No slumber party is complete without a little bit of fashion. Whether you want to dress like Lela and the biker girls or the coolest popstar, you can be whatever you want to be!

DESIGN AN OUTFIT FOR YOURSELF HERE.

DRAW YOU AND YOUR FRIENDS IN 1960S FASHIONS, LIKE LELA AND THE GANG!

Fab Friends, Fab Photos

STICK PHOTOS OF YOU AND YOUR BEST FRIENDS ON THESE PAGES.

GUESS WHO?

How well do you know your best friend? Fill in these details about them, then ask your friend for their answers to see if you were right!

FULL NAME:

_____

_____

DO THEY HAVE ANY BROTHERS OR SISTERS?

_____

WHAT IS HIS OR HER FAVOURITE MOVIE?

_____

_____

WHICH COLOUR IS THEIR FAVOURITE?
_____

HOW OLD ARE THEY?
_____
_____

WHAT ARE THEY MOST AFRAID OF?
_____
_____

WHAT IS THEIR DREAM?
_____
_____
_____

SO SURPRISED!

What things about your BFF surprised you after you got to know them? Write them down here.

NAME: _____

NICKNAME: _____

WHAT I KNEW ABOUT THEM WHEN WE FIRST MET:

_____

_____

_____

_____

_____

SOMETHING I KNOW ABOUT THEM NOW THAT SURPRISED ME:

_____

_____

_____

_____

_____

_____

_____

_____

_____

RHYME Time!

"Can I write a song for you?"

Write one line of a song for each of your friends, then sing it to them!

_____

_____

_____

_____

_____

_____

_____

_____

_____

_____

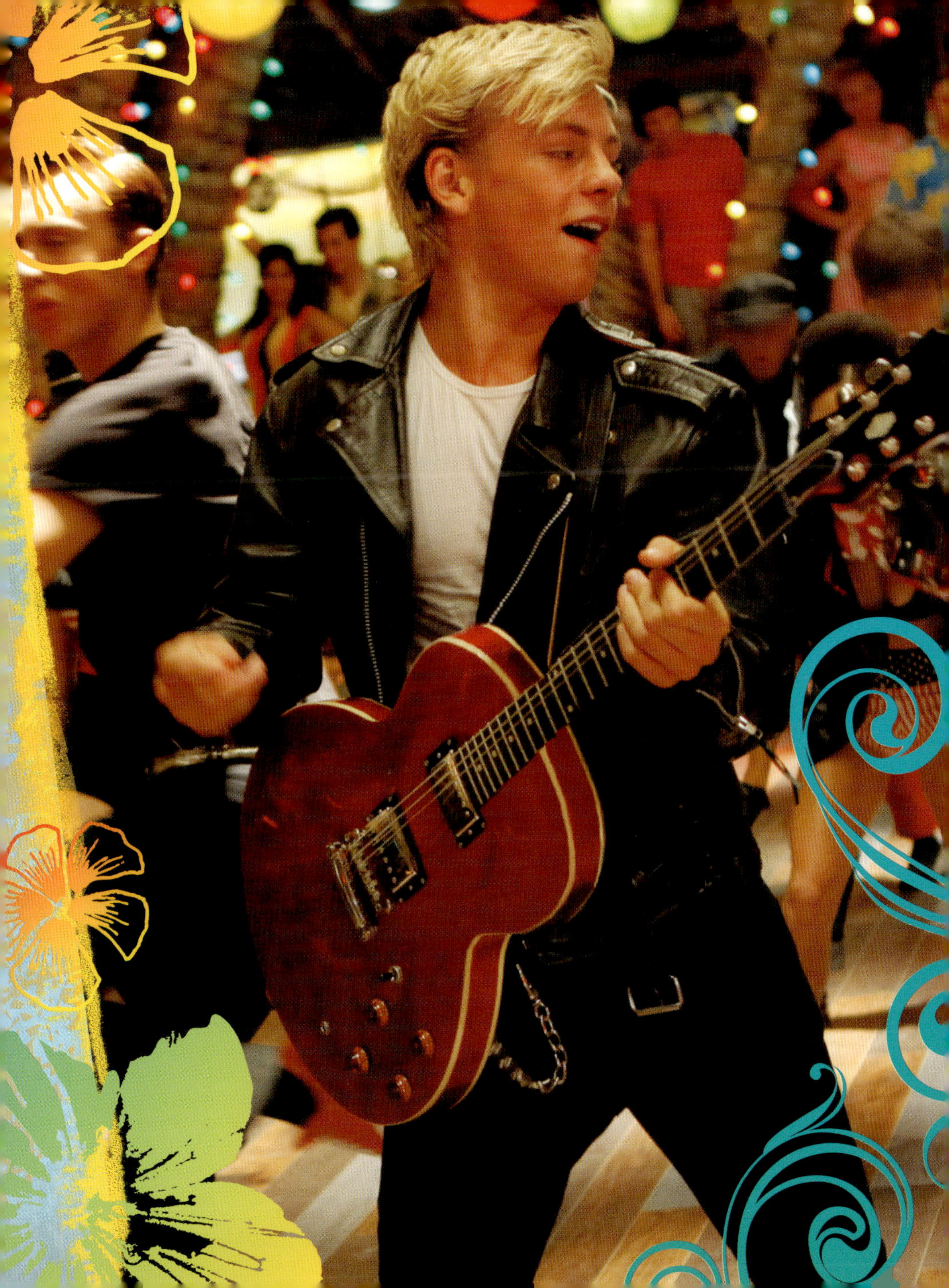

TOTALLY *Secret*

Mack's a great friend for listening to Lela's secret. Write all about your own top-secret stuff here.

WHAT'S THE BIGGEST SECRET YOU'VE SHARED?

_____
_____
_____
_____
_____

HAVE YOU EVER SPILLED SOMEONE ELSE'S SECRET?

_____
_____
_____

WHAT'S A SECRET YOU'RE GOING TO TELL YOUR BFF?

_____

_____

_____

_____

_____

WHAT'S THE SILLIEST SECRET YOU'VE TOLD?

_____

_____

_____

_____

ALWAYS SUMMER

Ahh summer holidays! Mack loves to spend her summer riding huge waves and hanging out with Brady at the beach. If you could plan the perfect summer, what would you do? Who would you hang out with? Write about it here.

YOU DEFINITELY SHOULD SURF

be Anything you want to Be

Mack faced some challenges before she realized she could be anything she wanted. List five things that challenge you that you've never told anyone about.

1. _____
2. _____
3. _____
4. _____
5. _____

When I grow up I want to be:

_____

_____

_____

_____

_____

_____

"It's your life. You should decide what you do!"

FOLLOW YOUR *Heart*

"People who don't follow their hearts leave their hearts behind."

WOULD YOU LEAVE YOUR HEART BEHIND OR FOLLOW IT? FIND OUT IN THIS QUIZ. CIRCLE TRUE OR FALSE FOR EACH STATEMENT, THEN CHECK YOUR RESULTS TO REVEAL YOUR DESTINY.

1. IF MY FRIENDS SAID MY DREAM WAS STUPID, THEN I WOULD GIVE IT UP.

    TRUE   FALSE

2. THERE SEEMS TO BE TOO MANY CHALLENGES – I SHOULD GET A NEW DREAM.

    TRUE   FALSE

3. ONLY BOYS CAN BE WHAT I WANT TO BE.

TRUE   FALSE

4. EVERYONE I KNOW HAS THE SAME DREAM. THAT'S HOW I CHOSE MINE.

TRUE   FALSE

5. IF I CAN'T ACHIEVE MY DREAM, THEN I'LL JUST DO SOMETHING ELSE.

TRUE   FALSE

IF YOU ANSWERED ...

MOSTLY TRUE: *Leave your dream behind*
If you're willing to give up your dream because of what someone said, or because you aren't that sure about it, then maybe it isn't your dream. Don't worry, maybe you just haven't found yours yet!

MOSTLY FALSE: *Your dream is where your heart is*
Congratulations, dreamer! It looks like nothing can stand between you and your dream. Just keep smiling through the hard bits along the way, and you'll reach your destiny.

FISH OUT OF WATER

Have you ever felt like you didn't belong somewhere? Write about it here:

80

Top Tips

If you've ever felt like you didn't fit in, then keep reading. Here are some secrets on how to not feel like an outsider.

KEEP YOUR COOL: Don't worry what everyone thinks about what you're wearing or what your hair looks like. Be confident in who you are and you'll feel at ease.

BE ANYTHING YOU WANT TO BE: You don't need to change your dreams or what you want to do just because you feel like you don't fit in. If the people you're hanging around with don't respect that, then find some friends that do!

JUST BE YOU: Pretending to be something you're not will only make you feel uncomfortable. If you keep true to yourself, then people will like you for you!

Secret Crush

Have you ever had a crush?
Write their name here:

_____

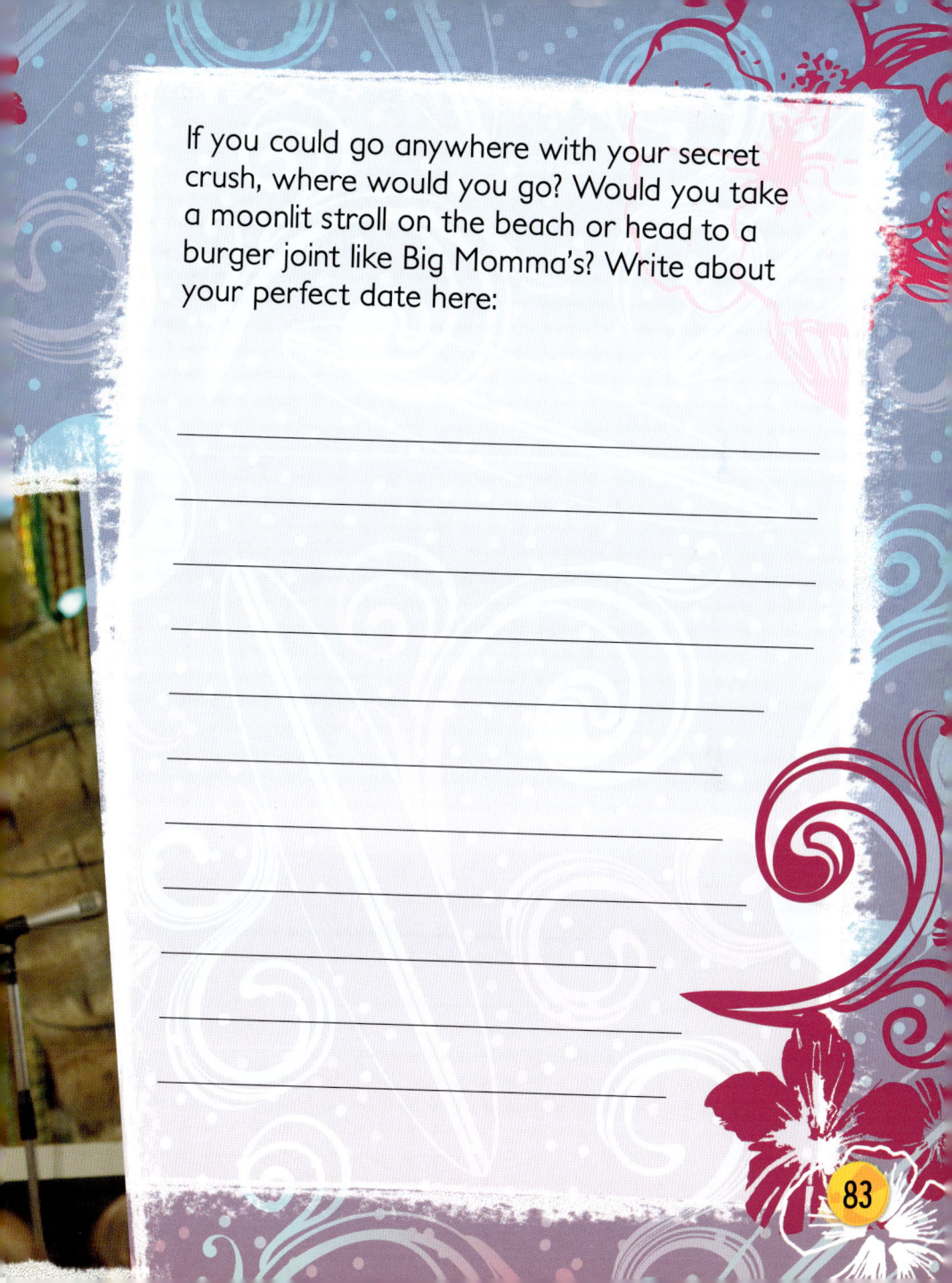

If you could go anywhere with your secret crush, where would you go? Would you take a moonlit stroll on the beach or head to a burger joint like Big Momma's? Write about your perfect date here:

_____

_____

_____

_____

_____

_____

_____

_____

_____

EAT, *hang*, SURF

WHAT ARE THE TOP THREE THINGS YOU LIKE TO DO? LIST THEM HERE.

RATE THESE THINGS FROM 1-10
(10 IS THE WORST AND 1 IS THE BEST)

RIDING A BIKE ....

HANGING OUT WITH FRIENDS ....

SINGING MY FAVE SONG ....

RIDING A WAVE ....

DOING HOMEWORK ....

PAINTING ....

CLEANING MY ROOM ....

DANCING ....

GOING TO A SLUMBER PARTY ....

DAYDREAMING ....

Girls can do *anything* boys can do

Mack teaches her new friends that girls can do all the things boys can do. What things do you think girls can do just as well as boys – if not better?!

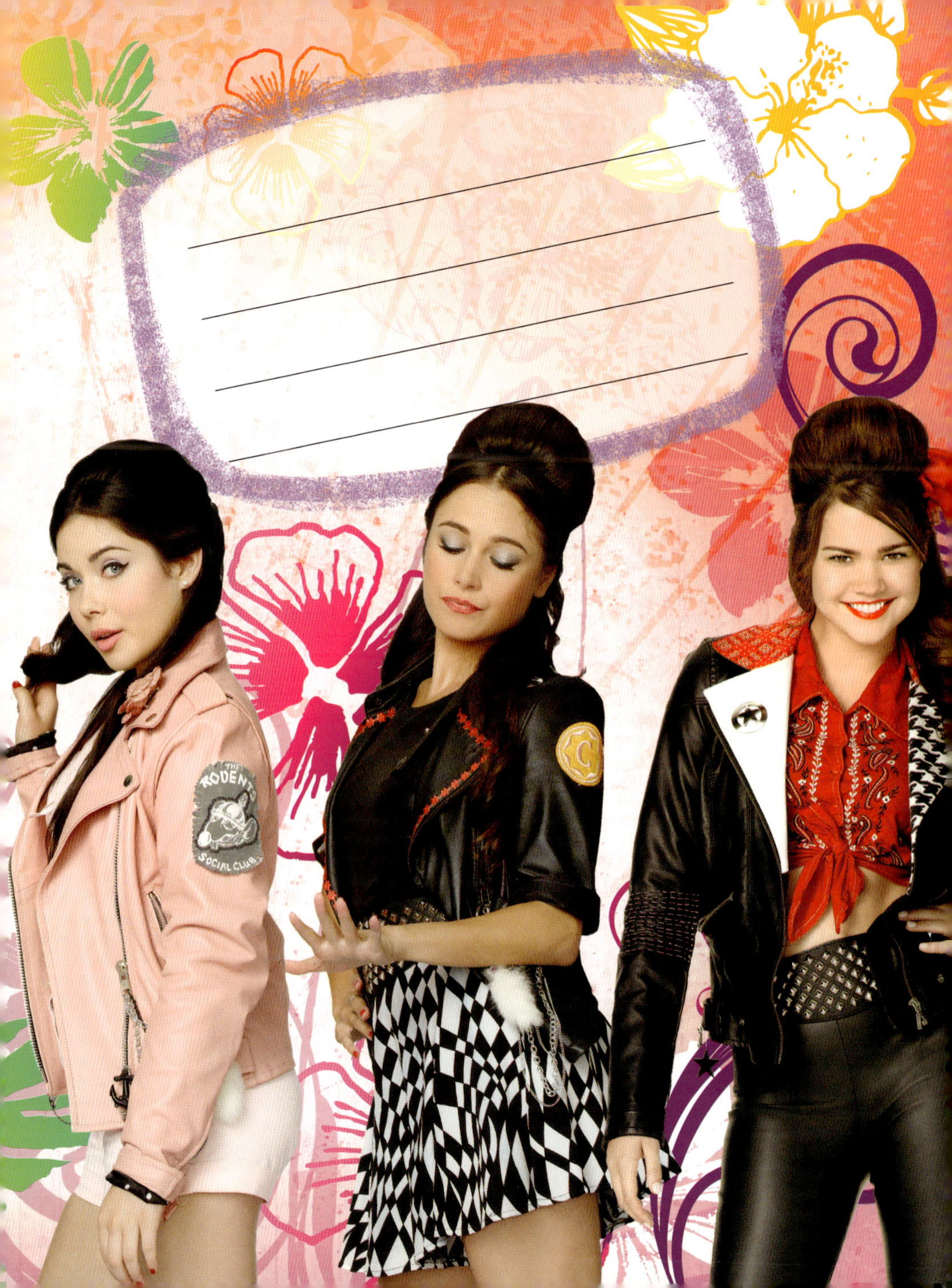
THE
RODENTS
SOCIAL CLUB

GET into the GROOVE

The bikers and the surfers know how to move! What's your dance style?

Score each statement from one to five. One means not true at all and five means very true! Then see how you measure up on the dance floor.

- IF YOUR FAVE SONG CAME ON IN A SHOP, YOU WOULD BUST OUT YOUR BEST MOVES, RIGHT THERE AND THEN. ☐

- YOU LOVE MOVIES AND TV PROGRAMMES THAT INVOLVE DANCING (IT'S THE BEST PART OF THE SHOW)! ☐

- YOU LOVE TO MAKE UP A NEW DANCE ROUTINE TO SHARE WITH YOUR FRIENDS. ☐

- YOU'D RATHER MAKE UP YOUR OWN STEPS THAN STICK TO THE CLASSIC ONES. ☐

- DANCING WITH YOUR FRIENDS IS SO MUCH FUN! ☐

YOUR RESULTS!

1-8: CHILLED-OUT CHICK
Your style is to go with the flow. You might not have a number ready to perform on the spot, but you can join in any dance scene and have a great time.

9-17: FAR-OUT FOOTWORK
You love dancing with your friends. When you hit the dance floor with some seriously cool moves, everyone wants to join in the fun!

18-25: GROOVY GIRL
Spin into the spotlight, dancing diva! If there's a beat, you just have to move to it — anytime, anywhere.

MAKE A MEMORY BOX

Summer's not over yet!

Keep hold of your memories by creating a memory box with your most treasured secrets.

HOW TO MAKE YOUR MEMORY BOX:

Grab a box — even a shoebox will do. Fill it with things that you treasure and want to remember always. Then tuck it away in a safe place. Many years from now, you'll be glad you kept those things!

WHAT ARE YOUR FAVOURITE MEMORIES?
_____
_____
_____
_____

WHICH OF YOUR THINGS DO YOU TREASURE THE MOST?
_____
_____
_____
_____
_____

YOU DEFINITELY SHOULD SURF

That was awesome!

You've revealed your wildest secrets and met the TEEN BEACH MOVIE gang – now complete this page!

My favourite page of this gnarly book was:
_____

The page I found hardest to complete was:
_____

My favourite Teen Beach Movie character is:
_____

Circle your answer!

I am a:

biker / surfer